OBJECTS IN SPACE

SATELLITES

by Ruth Owen

PowerKiDS press

New York

Published in 2015 by **The Rosen Publishing Group, Inc.**
29 East 21st Street, New York, NY 10010

Library of Congress Cataloging-in-Publication Data
Owen, Ruth.
Satellites / by Ruth Owen.
p. cm. — (Objects in space)
Includes index.
ISBN 978-1-4777-5859-5 (pbk.)
ISBN 978-1-4777-5858-8 (6-pack)
ISBN 978-1-4777-5856-4 (library binding)
1. Artificial satellites — Juvenile literature.
I. Owen, Ruth, 1967-. II. Title.
TL796.3 O94 2015
629.46—d23

Produced for Rosen by Ruby Tuesday Books Ltd
Editor for Ruby Tuesday Books Ltd: Mark J. Sachner
US Editor: Sara Antill
Designer: Emma Randall
Consultant: Kevin Yates, Fellow of the Royal Astronomical Society

Photo Credits:
Cover, 1, 25 © European Space Agency (ESA); 5, 7, 9 (bottom), 13, 15, 17,
19, 20–21, 23, 27 (bottom) © NASA; 9 (top), 26, 27 (top) © Shutterstock; 11
© Gregory R. Todd; 29 © Science Photo Library.

Manufactured in the United States of America
CPSIA Compliance Information: Batch # CW15PK: For Further Information contact
Rosen Publishing, New York, New York at 1-800-237-9932

CONTENTS

WATCHING AND LEARNING

Day and night, they travel around and around our Earth. Some are hundreds of miles (km) above Earth's surface. Others are **orbiting**, or circling, our planet many thousands of miles (km) away. They are **satellites**, and without them, we would know far less about the **universe**, and in many ways, our modern lives would not be possible.

A satellite is an object that orbits, or moves around, another object in space. A satellite can be natural. For example, the Moon is a satellite of Earth. A satellite can also be a human-made machine. Today, there are thousands of **artificial**, or human-made, satellites orbiting Earth. Some look beyond our **atmosphere** into space, investigating our **solar system**, our **galaxy**, and the universe beyond.

Others are pointed toward Earth. Some of these satellites help us get from point A to point B or help scientists predict the weather. Some transmit TV signals, while others make billions of cell phone calls possible every day. There are even satellites that are helping us protect our planet.

SPACE OBJECTS FACT FILE

Launched in 1957, the first satellite in space was the **Soviet Union's** *Sputnik 1*. In 1958, **NASA** launched *Explorer 1*, the United States' first satellite. In 1959, *Explorer 6* captured the first-ever satellite picture of Earth.

This photo of Earth was taken by *Explorer 6* on August 14, 1959. The picture is of the Pacific Ocean under clouds. At the time, the satellite was 17,000 miles (27,000 km) above Mexico.

The *Explorer 6* satellite.

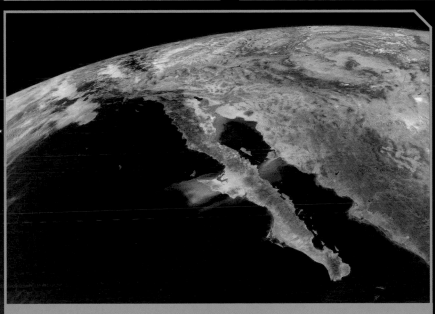

This image of the Pacific Ocean shows the Baja Peninsula and west coast of Mexico, as well as parts of the U.S. Southwest. It was taken by NASA's *Aqua* satellite on November 27, 2011.

SATELLITES IN ORBIT

Satellites come in many different sizes and shapes. They also move around Earth in many different orbits.

Some satellites orbit in a Low Earth Orbit (LEO). These satellites orbit at heights of up to 1,243 miles (2,000 km) above Earth's surface. Others are in a Medium Earth Orbit (MEO) at heights above LEO up to 22,236 miles (35,786 km), or High Earth Orbit (HEO), at heights above 22,236 miles (35,786 km).

Some satellites orbit at a distance of 26,199 miles (42,164 km) over Earth's equator. At this height, a satellite orbits at exactly the same rate as the Earth is spinning. This is called a geosynchronous orbit (GSO) because the satellite is synchronized with Earth's rotation.

Satellites that orbit from north to south are in a polar orbit. These types of satellites can orbit Earth in less than two hours. As the planet spins beneath it, the satellite views a different "strip" of Earth on each orbit, allowing it to see several sections, or strips, of Earth in a day.

SPACE OBJECTS FACT FILE

With so many satellites in space, collisions have to be avoided. Space organizations and satellite companies launch their satellites into orbital pathways that avoid other satellites. Then they track the satellites to make sure their orbits do not change.

A polar orbit

An illustration of the *Orbiting Carbon Observatory 2* satellite (launched in 2014). It is monitoring the amount of harmful carbon dioxide in Earth's atmosphere.

THE FIRST SATELLITE

On October 4, 1957, scientists from the Soviet Union launched *Sputnik 1*. The beach ball–sized object became the first-ever artificial satellite in space. The space age had begun!

Sputnik 1 was an aluminum sphere with a diameter of 23 inches (58 cm). It weighed 184 pounds (83 kg). The satellite was powered by three batteries and had four radio **antennae** that transmitted radio pulses, or beeps, into space.

Sputnik 1 was launched on a rocket from the region of the Soviet Union that is today the independent country of Kazakhstan. Once in orbit, *Sputnik 1* traveled through space at about 18,000 miles per hour (29,000 km/h). Each complete orbit of Earth took just over 96 minutes.

Astronomers and space enthusiasts around the world scanned the sky with telescopes and binoculars to watch for *Sputnik 1*. People with radio equipment listened for the satellite's "beep, beep" as it passed over their part of the world.

SPACE OBJECTS FACT FILE

When translated, the Russian word "sputnik" originally meant "fellow traveler." In the decades since the launch of *Sputnik 1*, however, the word has come to mean "satellite" in the Russian language.

4 ОКТЯБРЯ
1957 г.

40 коп. Первый в мире советский искусственный спутник Земли

ПОЧТА СССР

A Soviet Union stamp showing *Sputnik 1's* orbit.

A technician puts the finishing touches on *Sputnik 1*, the world's first artificial satellite.

Antenna

SPUTNIK 1

Sputnik 1's mission had several scientific goals.

Testing if it was possible first to launch a satellite into orbit around Earth and then to track the satellite were two of the mission's goals. Finding out if a satellite could function and transmit radio signals in space was key, too. Sputnik 1 also supplied scientists on Earth with information about Earth's atmosphere.

Sputnik 1 transmitted radio beeps for 22 days until its batteries ran out of power. It then continued to orbit Earth until January 1958. During its time in space, it traveled 43.5 million miles (70 million km). On January 4, 1958, Sputnik 1 fell from orbit and burned up in Earth's atmosphere.

To be the country that sent the first artificial satellite into space was a huge achievement for the Soviet Union. The United States did not want to be left behind. Sputnik 1's launch led to the space race, a competition between the Soviet Union and the United States to become the dominant, most successful nation in space exploration.

SPACE OBJECTS FACT FILE

Sputnik 1's successful mission inspired many people to become space scientists and **engineers**. Some were even inspired to become astronauts.

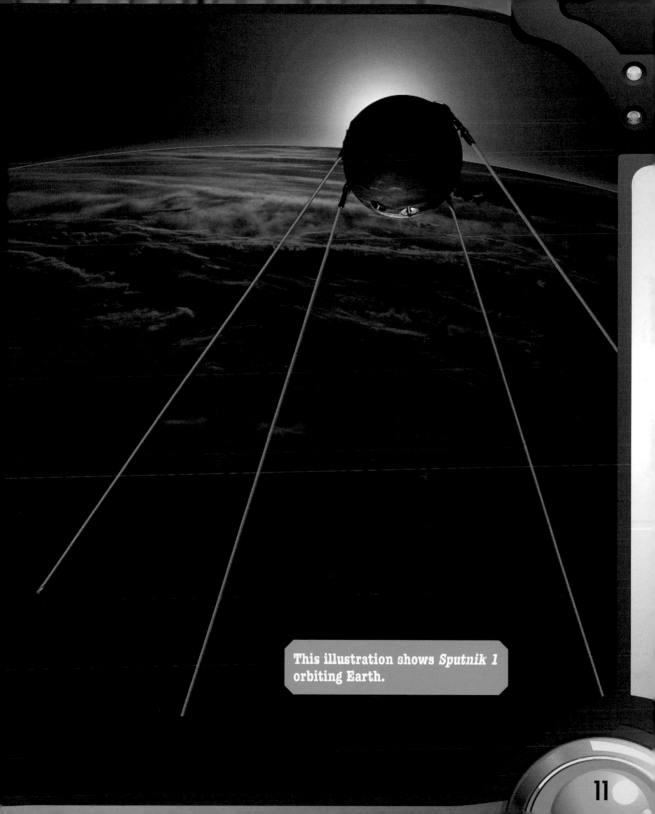

This illustration shows *Sputnik 1* orbiting Earth.

THE HUBBLE SPACE TELESCOPE

Since *Sputnik 1* made its pioneering voyage into space, thousands of satellites have left Earth. One of the most famous satellites currently studying space is the Hubble Space Telescope built by NASA and the European Space Agency (ESA).

Telescopes on Earth can see far into space. A satellite telescope, such as the Hubble, flies above Earth's atmosphere. This allows it to see distant objects in space more clearly because the gases and dust in our atmosphere do not blur its view.

Hubble was launched on April 24, 1990. It was carried into space aboard the space shuttle *Discovery* and placed into orbit by the shuttle's robotic arm. Unfortunately, scientists on Earth soon discovered a tiny but catastrophic problem with the telescope, which meant its images were blurred. In 1993, the space shuttle *Endeavour* flew a mission to repair the Hubble. The telescope was captured by the shuttle's robot arm and, as the shuttle and telescope orbited Earth, astronauts made spacewalks to carry out repairs.

The repaired Hubble went on to produce truly stunning images that wow astronomers and the general public to this day.

SPACE OBJECTS FACT FILE

The Hubble Space Telescope is named after Edwin P. Hubble, an American astronomer who discovered many galaxies. His work also showed that since the universe came into being, billions of years ago, it has been expanding, or growing bigger.

Discovery's robotic arm

The Hubble Space Telescope is released into space.

The Hubble Space Telescope lifts off safely packed inside the cargo bay of *Discovery*.

A TELESCOPE WITH WOW FACTOR

For more than 20 years, the Hubble Space Telescope has been orbiting Earth. The school bus–sized satellite travels at around 5 miles per second (8 km/s).

Hubble captures images of planets, stars, and galaxies. It has helped scientists understand what happens when a star dies in a huge explosion called a **supernova**. It has shown us beautiful **nebulae**, which are massive clouds of gas and dust where stars form.

Hubble has helped scientists learn how galaxies form. It has even helped them understand the formation of the universe and come to the conclusion that it was formed 13 to 14 billion years ago.

Hubble's images have taught us a vast amount about space. They have also shown us how beautiful the universe is!

SPACE OBJECTS FACT FILE

Hubble stores its images and other data on board. Then, twice a day, the images and data are transmitted via a group of other satellites to large, dish-shaped, ground-based antennae, or terminals, in White Sands, New Mexico. Scientists then use computers to turn Hubble's raw images into stunning pictures.

This Hubble picture is called "Hubble Ultra Deep Field." It shows about 10,000 galaxies. Some of the galaxies are the oldest ever seen. They formed when the universe was still young.

Hubble captured this image of the Butterfly Nebula. The two "wings" are massive clouds of gas heated to more than 36,000°F (20,000°C).

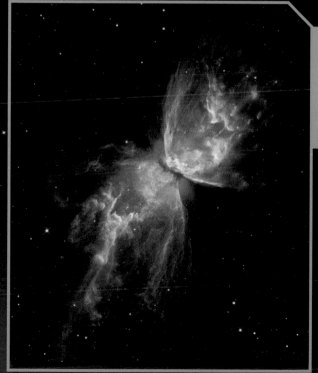

SEARCHING FOR ASTEROIDS

On December 14, 2009, NASA's Wide-field Infrared Survey Explorer (WISE) satellite was launched.

The WISE telescope searches space and captures images using infrared light. This type of light, or energy, cannot be seen with the human eye in the way that visible light can. WISE is able to see and photograph very distant or dark objects that cannot be seen with visible light. During the first two years of its mission, WISE photographed 560 million objects including galaxies, **comets**, and **asteroids**. It captured 7,500 images each day. The satellite discovered more than 34,000 asteroids in the **asteroid belt** between Mars and Jupiter. It also discovered 21 comets.

In 2013, WISE was renamed NEOWISE and began a new three-year mission to look for **Near-Earth Objects (NEOs)**. An NEO is an asteroid or comet that comes close to Earth's orbit. Once discovered, an NEO is observed so its future pathway can be calculated and any threat to Earth can be ruled out.

SPACE OBJECTS FACT FILE

In December 2013, NEOWISE discovered a previously unknown Near-Earth Object (NEO), asteroid 2013 YP 139. The asteroid is just under half a mile (0.8 km) wide. In about 100 years, it will pass within 300,000 miles (480,000 km) of Earth.

The Wide-field Infrared Survey Explorer (WISE) satellite ready to begin its mission.

Using data from **NEOWISE**, scientists created this image. It shows the estimated number of NEO asteroids near Earth's orbit (shown in green).

The orange dots show Potentially Hazardous Asteroids (PHAs), asteroids with orbits that will bring them closest to Earth's orbit. PHAs are large enough to survive entry through Earth's atmosphere.

FAST-MOVING SWIFT

SWIFT is a satellite launched by NASA in November 2004. It searches the sky for gamma ray bursts.

Gamma ray bursts are the brightest, most energetic explosions in the universe. They happen when a star dies, or explodes, in a supernova or hypernova, which is an especially high-energy supernova. A gamma ray burst can last for just a fraction of a second or for several minutes. Then it fades very quickly.

SWIFT's Burst Alert Telescope can view one-sixth of space at any one time. When it detects a gamma ray burst, it turns its instruments toward the burst within seconds. An alert also goes out to astronomers on Earth day or night. Then other space telescopes and ground-based telescopes can be turned toward the burst to study the explosion and its afterglow.

SWIFT's data allows scientists to find out how bright gamma ray bursts are and how far away from Earth they are happening. Information gathered during the afterglow allows scientists to study the region of space where the gamma ray burst took place.

SPACE OBJECTS FACT FILE

The SWIFT satellite was named for its ability to quickly turn and change position, just like swifts, which are small birds that can instantly change direction in mid-flight.

This illustration shows SWIFT and a gamma ray burst.

Ursa Major

Leo

GRB 130427A

On April 27, 2013, SWIFT detected the brightest gamma ray burst yet observed, GRB 130427A. These sky maps show an area of space before (left) and during the burst (right).

LOOKING BACK IN TIME

Hubble, NEOWISE, and others are telling us much about our universe. In the future, they will be joined by even more powerful space telescopes.

The giant James Webb Space Telescope (JWST) will be launched in 2018. Its mission is to help scientists understand how stars, planets, and galaxies first formed.

All telescopes act like time machines, collecting light that left objects many years ago. The universe has been expanding ever since it formed, which means the other galaxies are moving away from us. The farther across the universe a telescope can see, the farther back in time it is looking. JWST will be able to collect light that left galaxies and stars billions of years ago, when the universe was still very young.

By the time such ancient light reaches us across the continually expanding universe, it is no longer seen as visible light. It has been stretched along the way and is now seen at the longer wavelength of infrared light. Human eyes cannot see infrared light, but JWST can.

JWST will also be able to see through the dust that makes up nebulae to see stars forming. This is because infrared light is not obscured by dust.

An illustration of the James Webb Space Telescope.

Scientists carry out tests on six of the hexagonal sections that will make up the Webb's mirror.

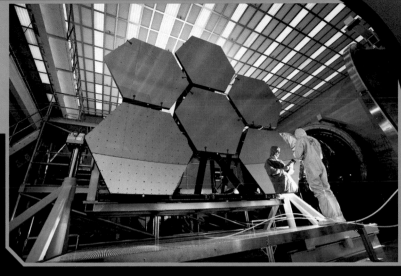

The mirror is made up of 18 hexagonal sections.

SPACE OBJECTS FACT FILE

All telescopes have a mirror. In order to capture very distant, faint objects, the James Webb Space Telescope needs an enormous mirror. Scientists had to figure out how such a large mirror could fit on the rocket that will launch the telescope. They designed a mirror made up of 18 tight-fitting hexagonal sections that can be collapsed and folded for the journey.

THE JAMES WEBB SPACE TELESCOPE

In order to observe space in infrared light, the James Webb Space Telescope must be kept very cool. It cannot be heated by light from the Sun or by reflected light from Earth and the Moon.

A large sun shield on JWST will protect the telescope from heat. Unusually, the telescope will not orbit Earth, but will travel around a point in space named Lagrange 2 (L2). This orbital position was chosen because at this point, the telescope's shield will offer protection from the Sun, Earth, and Moon no matter where in their orbits the three objects are.

The infrared images from JWST will be beautiful and very high quality. When they are first beamed back to Earth, however, they won't mean much to our eyes. Using computers, scientists will turn the infrared images into beautiful, Hubble-like pictures of the universe that will show us stars, nebulae, and galaxies.

SPACE OBJECTS FACT FILE

The James Webb Space Telescope is named after NASA's James E. Webb. In the 1960s, Webb played an important role in the development of the Apollo program that sent astronauts to the Moon. Space agencies from around the world are working together to build and operate the telescope.

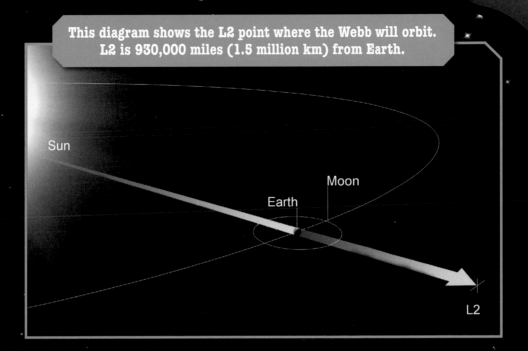

This diagram shows the L2 point where the Webb will orbit.
L2 is 930,000 miles (1.5 million km) from Earth.

Sun

Moon

Earth

L2

Scientists work on a test version of the sun shield for the
James Webb Space Telescope.

CRYOSAT-2

Not all satellites look out into space. Many are studying our own planet, Earth.

The European Space Agency's *CryoSat-2* is the size of a large car. Its mission is to measure the thickness of floating sea ice and the vast ice sheets that cover places such as Antarctica and Greenland.

The satellite does this by precisely measuring the height of the ice. By comparing each year's data to previous years, scientists can calculate if the ice is getting thinner or thicker. This is important work because ice at Earth's poles is melting as temperatures rise due to **climate change**. When ice in the Arctic and Antarctic melts, the water enters the ocean and contributes to rising sea levels.

CryoSat-2's instruments send radar pulses toward the ice. A pulse bounces off the ice and back to the satellite. The time it takes for the pulse to return is measured. If the time is longer than from the previous year, it means the ice is not as high, or thick.

SPACE OBJECTS FACT FILE

In 2012, *CryoSat-2* took more than 68 million measurements from the ice sheets in Greenland and Antarctica. The measurements showed 300 cubic miles (500 cubic km) of ice had been lost.

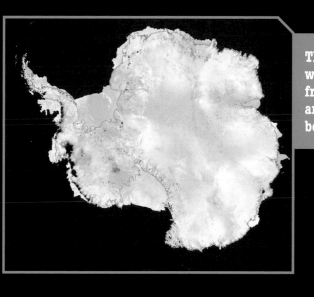

This image of Antarctica was created using data from *CryoSat-2*. The red areas are where the ice has become thinner.

This illustration shows *CryoSat-2*. It orbits Earth's poles at an average height of 450 miles (724 km) above the surface.

SATELLITES IN OUR WORLD

Most satellites don't have a name we would recognize, like "Hubble." We would miss these satellites, however, if they weren't there!

Satellites make TV, radio, the Internet, and cell phone calls possible. Signals from TV stations or a person's cell phone must travel in a straight line—they can't curve around a mountain or tall building. By using satellites, a signal is transmitted from one point on Earth up to a communications satellite. Then the satellite instantly beams the signal back down to its destination point.

If you're lost on a mountain or can't find a street in a city, a satellite global positioning system (GPS) can help you via a GPS receiving device such as a cell phone, special watch, or in-car system. A GPS device listens for signals from several satellites. Then, based on its position in relation to the satellites, the device figures out where in the world it is. The device then gives you this information, and can also give you detailed directions or a map to follow.

A hiker checks his location using a GPS device.

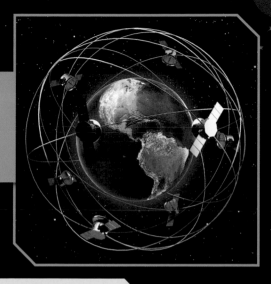

This illustration shows how global positioning system satellites orbit Earth.

SPACE OBJECTS FACT FILE

From high above Earth, weather satellites photograph and collect data on clouds, winds, thunderstorms, hurricanes, and other types of weather. For example, satellites can show scientists the size of a hurricane and the direction in which it is traveling.

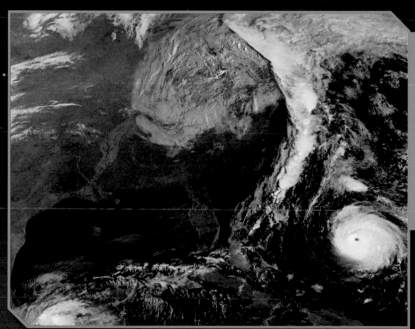

The GOES-East weather satellite captured this image of Hurricane Gonzalo (bottom right) off the east coast of the United States in October 2014.

HELP IN A DISASTER

A satellite is able to see a large area of Earth at one time. It can capture images and collect data fast in a way that would be impossible from the ground. These abilities make satellites an essential tool for organizations that respond to disasters.

The Disaster Monitoring Constellation for International Imaging (DMCii) is a group of satellites that are currently orbiting Earth. They are jointly operated by six countries, including the United Kingdom and China.

When a disaster such as an earthquake, tsunami, flood, forest fire, or volcanic eruption happens, the DMCii satellites can be directed to take detailed photos of the situation on the ground. This information can then be sent to a country's government and rescue services within 24 hours. The images show emergency services the size of a disaster and where best to target their help. The satellites can then continue to capture images every day to monitor how the situation is developing.

SPACE OBJECTS FACT FILE

The DMCii satellites also keep watch over rain forests. They capture images of vast areas of forest on a regular basis. This allows conservation groups and governments to see if trees are being cut down illegally.

This satellite image shows the Japanese town of Rikuzentakata on the east coast of Japan in July 2010.

This satellite image shows Rikuzentakata in March 2011 after a devastating tsunami hit Japan. Images like these can be used in responding to disasters.

GLOSSARY

antennae
(an-TEN-ee) Parts of a machine or device that pick up radio signals. Also known as aerials.

artificial
(ar-ti-FISH-uhl) Not natural; made by people.

asteroid belt
(AS-teh-royd BELT) A region of the solar system between the orbits of Mars and Jupiter where the largest number of known asteroids orbit the Sun.

asteroids
(AS-teh-roydz) Rocky objects orbiting the Sun and ranging in size from a few feet (m) to hundreds of miles (km) in diameter.

atmosphere
(AT-muh-sfeer) The layer of gases surrounding a planet, moon, or star.

climate change
(KLY-mut CHAYNJ) A change in Earth's temperatures and weather that takes place gradually over a long time period.

comets
(KAH-mitz) Objects orbiting the Sun consisting of a center of ice and dust and, when near the Sun, tails of gas and dust particles.

engineers
(en-jun-NIHRZ) People who use math, science, and technology to design and build machines such as cars and spacecraft. Some engineers design and build structures such as skyscrapers and bridges.

galaxy
(GA-lik-see) A group of stars, dust, gas, and other objects held together in outer space by gravity.

NASA
(NAS-ah) The National Aeronautics and Space Administration, an organization in the United States that studies space and builds spacecraft.

Near-Earth Objects (NEOs)
(NEER URTH OB-jekts) Asteroids or comets that come within 28 million miles (45 million km) of the Earth's orbit around the Sun.

nebulae
(NEB-yoo-lee) Massive clouds of gas and dust in outer space. Stars form in a nebula.

orbiting
(OR-bih-ting) Moving, or traveling, around another object in a curved path.

satellites
(SA-tih-lytz) Objects that orbit another object in space, such as a planet. A satellite may be naturally occurring, such as a moon, or an artificial satellite used for transmitting television or cell phone signals.

solar system
(SOH-ler SIS-tem) The Sun and everything that orbits around it, including planets and their moons, asteroids, meteoroids, and comets.

Soviet Union
(SOH-vee-et YOON-yun) A former nation made up of a group of republics in parts of Europe and Asia. The Soviet Union broke up in 1991, creating a group of independent nations, including Russia, Ukraine, Kazakhstan, and Georgia.

supernova
(soo-per-NOH-vuh) A super-bright explosion of a star that creates a sudden release of energy and light. Its remains may form nebulae.

universe
(YOO-nih-vers) All of the matter and energy that exists as a whole, including gravity and all the planets, stars, galaxies, and contents of space.

WEBSITES

Due to the changing nature of Internet links, PowerKids Press has developed an online list of websites related to the subject of this book. This site is updated regularly. Please use this link to access the list: www.powerkidslinks.com/ois/sat

READ MORE

Fleisher, Paul. *Doppler Radar, Satellites, and Computer Models: The Science of Weather*. Minneapolis, MN: Lerner Publications, 2011.

Snedden, Robert. *Mapping Earth from Space*. Chicago: Raintree, 2011.

Zappa, Marcia. *Rockets and Satellites*. Edina, MN: ABDO Publishing, 2011.